DATE DUE

L'Chaim

The Story of a Russian Émigré Boy

TRICIA BROWN

Photographs by
KENNETH KOBRÉ

Henry Holt and Company • New York

The author and photographer gratefully acknowledge the following, whose knowledge, support, and encouragement made this book possible: the Marcel Tsukerman family; Rabbi Bentzion Pil and his family; the children and parents at the Beth Aharon Jewish Day School; Rabbi Yosef Langer, Chabad of San Francisco; Congregation Chevrat Thilim; The Jewish Education Center; Joyce Ahern, children's librarian, Jewish Community Library; Trude Lieser, Jewish Community Library; Barbara Goodman, Director, Holocaust Center; Carol Nemeroff, Principal, Brandeis Hillel Day School; Amy Talisman, Principal, Bessie Carmichael School; Tat Wong Kung Fu Academy; Natan's Glatt Kosher Foods; Znanie Book Store; Buffy Francisco, Ellie Sears, Aaron Sears, Reuben Sears, Betsy Brill, Patrick Kobré, Dennis Brill, Linda Bartling, Andrea Brown, Barrett Brown, and our wonderful editor, Simone Kaplan.

Henry Holt and Company, Inc.
Publishers since 1866
115 West 18th Street
New York, New York 10011

Henry Holt is a registered
trademark of Henry Holt and Company, Inc.

Published in Canada by Fitzhenry & Whiteside Ltd.,
195 Allstate Parkway, Markham, Ontario L3R 4T8.

Library of Congress Cataloging-in-Publication Data
Brown, Tricia.
    L'Chaim: the story of a Russian émigré boy /
by Tricia Brown; photographs by Kenneth Kobré.
    Includes bibliographical references.
    1. Jews, Russian—California—San Francisco—
Juvenile literature.   2. Jewish children—California—
San Francisco—Religious life—Juvenile literature.
3. Orthodox Judaism—Customs and practices—
Juvenile literature.   [1. Jews—Social life and customs.
2. Judaism—Customs and practices.
3. Russian Americans.]
I. Kobré, Kenneth, ill.   II. Title.
F869.S39J53   1994   979.4'61004924047—dc20
93-44853   ISBN 0-8050-2354-2

First Edition—1994

Printed in the United States of America
on acid-free paper. ∞
10 9 8 7 6 5 4 3 2 1

This book is dedicated to
Zev and his family;
Rabbi Pil and his family;
my son, Barrett; and
children of émigré families
everywhere . . . *l'chaim!*
                              —T. B.

To Dr. Sidney and Reva Kobré,
and my dear wife, Betsy
                              —K. K.

Foreword

Zev was born in Odessa on July 15, 1983. At that time, Odessa was a city in the state of the Ukraine in the Union of Soviet Socialist Republics, sometimes called Russia after the largest state in the union.

In 1991, the Ukraine became an independent nation—there is no longer a Union of Soviet Socialist Republics and Russia is itself a completely separate country. Zev and his family never refer to themselves as Ukrainians, though. They speak Russian and call themselves Russians, or, now that they have left, Russian émigrés. Sometimes they refer to their old home as Russia, sometimes as the Soviet Union. For these reasons, I have used both those names in this book.

As you will read, Zev and his family are Jewish. The Tsukermans were prevented from practicing their religion by the Soviet government, but they were classified as Jewish and always considered themselves to be so. When I asked Zev if he thought of himself as Ukrainian, he replied, "Oh, no! I always thought of myself as Jewish!"

Even so, when they arrived in America they knew nothing about their religion and had to learn all of it from the beginning. The fact that it was once all but impossible to practice makes it even more valuable to them. Now they are Orthodox Jews and observe all the traditional laws.

L'Chaim is the story of what Zev's life is like today, now that he is living in a country where he has the right to life, liberty, and the pursuit of happiness.

Tricia Brown

Hello, America! My name is Zev Tsukerman. I was born in Odessa in the Ukraine, which used to be part of the Union of Soviet Socialist Republics (USSR); but now my family and I live in San Francisco. We are émigrés, which means that we left the country of our birth for political reasons. In our case, the reasons were religious, too. My family is Jewish, and until recently Jews were not allowed to practice our religion in Ukraine. We moved to America because we wanted our religious freedom.

The United States Constitution gives you the right to practice any faith you want. It also assures your right to dress the way you want, eat the food you want, and celebrate any holidays you want. In our Declaration of Independence, it says every American has the right to "life, liberty and the pursuit of happiness." We didn't have these rights when we lived in the Soviet Union.

Now things have changed in my old country. The USSR broke up into separate countries. Ukraine declared its independence (just like the independence we celebrate here on the Fourth of July!). But even though this happened in 1991 and many changes have taken place, there is still a lot of prejudice against Jewish people in Ukraine.

Here in America we have the freedom to live our life as we wish. This has made us very happy. *L'chaim!* That means "To life!" in Hebrew, the language of Jews everywhere.

In this photo I am with my mother, my father, my grandparents, and my baby brother, Joshua. All of us came from the USSR except for my baby brother. He was born where we live now—in San Francisco. My grandparents live in another apartment a few blocks away from us. In Odessa, at least two families would live in a two-bedroom apartment like this.

Our faith, Judaism, is one of the oldest religions in the world. My family practices Orthodox Judaism, which means we accept all traditional Jewish beliefs and ways of life.

Here my mother is helping me put on my *tzitzis*. It looks like a white bib with fringes hanging from each of the four corners. Orthodox Jewish men wear these as a reminder of the 613 commandments they must follow. In some pictures in this book, you will be able to see the fringes hanging from under my clothes.

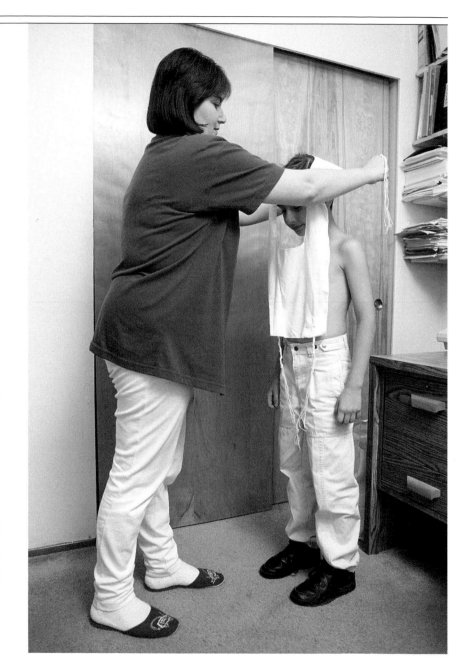

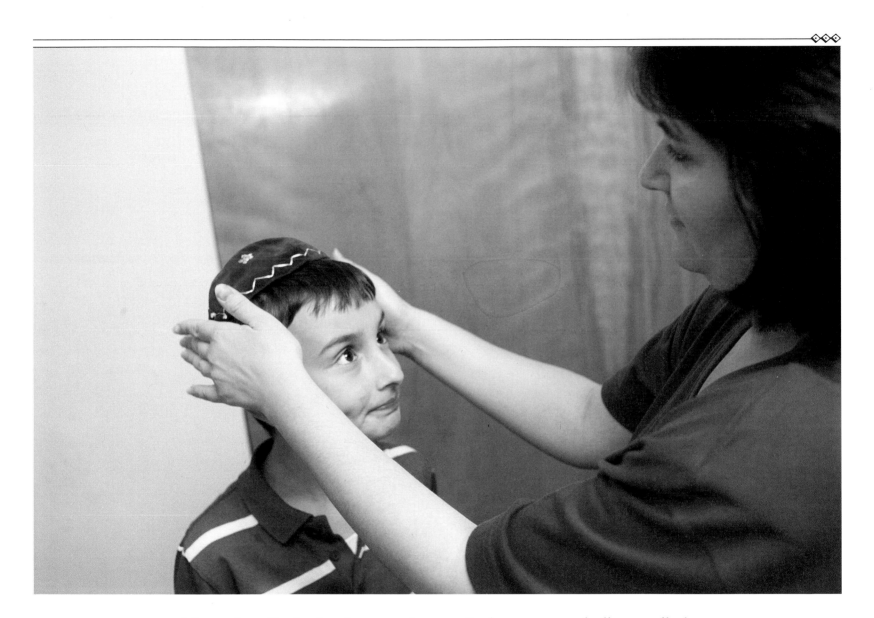

Like other Orthodox boys and men, I also wear a skullcap called a *yarmulke*. We wear our yarmulkes at all times as a sign of respect to God, and to remind us that he is there to guide us.

I attend Beth Aharon Jewish Day School, where I am in the fourth grade.
My teacher is Rabbi Levy.

A *rabbi* is a spiritual leader and an interpreter of Jewish law. A rabbi must study Hebrew sacred writings for many years.

Rabbi Levy teaches me the prayers I am supposed to know. This morning he asks me to recite the morning prayer.

Shhh . . . everyone is supposed to be quiet. . . .

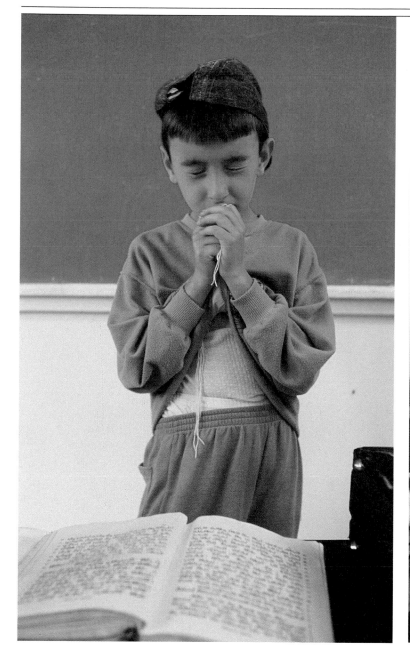

Hooray! Rabbi Levy said I did a good job with the prayers. I had to say them in Hebrew, and I didn't make one mistake!

Here is a picture of my best friend, Schneur. He is Rabbi Pil's son. You will meet Rabbi Pil when we go to the *synagogue,* our place of worship. Rabbi Pil is the only Russian-speaking rabbi in Northern California. One of his jobs is to teach the Russian Jews who come to this country how to practice their religion, since they weren't able to in their homeland.

Schneur will become a rabbi too. He takes special classes after school. Here he is helping me learn to read Hebrew. See how different the alphabet looks? We open a Hebrew book from what would be the back of an English book and we read from right to left.

In school we learn about all the Jewish holidays, customs, and traditions. Right now we are learning about *tzedoka*. In this picture I am waiting for my turn. See the red mushroom-shaped box? It is from Russia, and I use it as my tzedoka box. Tzedoka means charity. It reminds us that there are other people in the world less fortunate than ourselves who might need help. We give charity every day except on the *Shabbat* and on Jewish holidays.

Shabbat is our day of rest and worship. It begins on Friday, eighteen minutes before sundown, when candles are lit. In this photograph the girls in my class are practicing the lighting of the candles. At home my mother does this. After the candles are lit, she recites a special prayer. Shabbat is a day of rest and prayer, so Orthodox Jews go to synagogue on that day, and we do not travel, work, or carry money. Shabbat ends at sundown Saturday.

At my school we study the usual subjects too. I learn math, reading, writing, science, social studies, music, and art. In this picture my friend Max and I show off the self-portraits we painted in art.

Of course, we have my favorite subject—P.E. I like to play soccer a lot.
Dima likes to play tag, but he can't catch me—I'm too fast!

After school I do a lot of different things. Sometimes I play with my baby brother, but most of the time I play on my computer.

My dad is a computer programmer, so he has taught me a lot. I think I might work with computers when I grow up.

Once a week I go to my kung fu class. I am getting very strong, doing the exercises.

It's fun and I have made some new friends there. When I lived in the Soviet Union, there were no kung fu classes to take.

ЛИТЕРАТУР
ГАЗЕТА

СВОБО

1 сентября
1993 г.
№ 35 (5463)

Выходит по средам

Началась
подписка на
1-ое полугодие
1994 года!
Подписка
намного
дешевле,
чем
приобретение
«ЛГ» в розницу.

Вы

были многолетним подписчиком «Литературной :
Хотите вернуться к нам? Нет ничего проще. Под

недавно стали нашим читателем ".
Оставайтесь с нами и Вы не разоча
чем на другие издания

не знакомы с «Литгазетой»?
Вы много потеряли. В нашей газет
которых нет в других изданиях.
Раньше других газет, уже в среду,

Often in the afternoons I go shopping on Geary Street with my grandfather. Here there are several stores that sell Russian items. My grandfather goes into this store to pick up a Russian newspaper. Here it is. The Russian alphabet looks different from the English alphabet. It is called *Cyrillic*. I speak Russian with my grandfather and my parents sometimes, but mostly we speak English.

At this store I like to look at the *matrioshka* dolls. These are popular Russian toys. You open one and out pops a smaller one; you open that and out pops another; you open that and out pops another; and it keeps going that way until you come to the last one, a very tiny doll that can't be opened.

We also go food shopping when we are on Geary Street. We are careful to buy only foods that are *kosher*. All our food is prepared according to the dietary laws of Judaism, which are called the laws of *koshrut*. There are some foods we can't eat, and other foods must be prepared in a special way, especially meat. Since we weren't allowed to practice Judaism in the Soviet Union, we couldn't keep kosher there.

In this picture we are in a kosher butcher shop. One of the dietary laws says an animal intended for meat has to be killed in a very particular way—quickly and painlessly. Also, a special blessing is said during the slaughter.

Another of the dietary laws says we must keep meat and milk products separate and not serve them at the same meal. Orthodox Jews always keep kosher. It is one of the signs of our faith. Now that we have the freedom to practice our religion, we observe the laws wherever we are: at home, at school, even when visiting friends. It means I can't eat a hamburger or a hot dog at a restaurant that isn't kosher. Sometimes it's frustrating, but most times I don't mind. It's just the way I live my life.

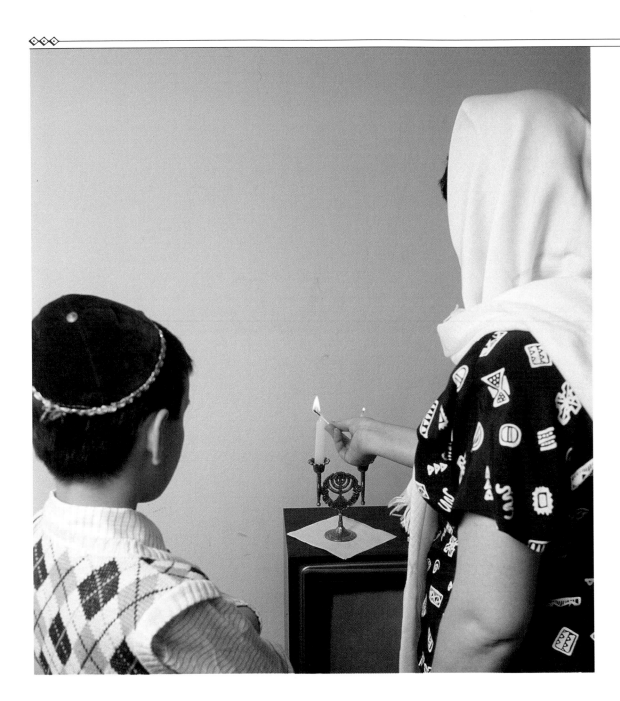

We observe many holidays in our religion. I already told you about the Shabbat, which occurs every week. Tonight's Shabbat is special, as it is the beginning of the Jewish New Year, which is called *Rosh Hashanah*. Rosh Hashanah falls on the first day of the first month called *Tishri* in the Hebrew calendar. The Hebrew calendar is based on the cycles of the moon, so the exact date of the celebration changes every year, but it always occurs during September or October.

Rosh Hashanah starts just as Shabbat does—with my mother lighting the candles and saying the blessing.

We sit down and my father says the blessing called the *kiddush* over a glass of wine and two loaves of special bread called *challah*. The bread is braided and smooth because it symbolizes the wish for a smooth year ahead.

We leave the table to have the ritual of the washing of hands. In this picture I'm helping my grandfather. Water is poured three times over the right hand and three times over the left hand while we say our prayers. We return to the table and do not speak until all the prayers have been said.

Some of the foods served during this meal have special meaning. Honey, symbolizing sweetness, is placed on the table. It is put on the bread, and apples are dipped in it so that there will be sweetness as well as fruitfulness in the New Year ahead.

Solemn services are held in the synagogue for the next two days. The part I like best is listening to the blowing of the *shofar.* This is a ram's horn that makes an eerie, hollow sound. It's supposed to remind us of great events in Jewish history and make us think about the importance of being good Jews. Jews believe that everybody was created in God's image and each of us deserves dignity and respect.

After the service Rabbi Pil lets me try to
blow the shofar. Whew! It is hard work.

Rosh Hashanah begins a period of ten days called the *Days of Awe*. During this time we are supposed to be quiet and think about any wrongdoing we may have done. I do my work quietly at school and think about what I can do better.

A reading in the Old Testament tells us to "cast our sins into the depths of the sea." So on Sunday my father takes my friends and me to the beach. My father likes swimming. It reminds him of when he was a boy in the Soviet Union and swam in the Black Sea. We like swimming too, but we don't forget the serious reason for being here.

The ten days of reflection end with *Yom Kippur.* In English it is called the *Day of Atonement.* This is the holiest day of the Jewish year and the day on which we ask forgiveness for all of our sins. On Yom Kippur everyone fasts except small children and sick people. Those people who fast do not eat or drink from sunset on one day to sunset on the following day.

At the synagogue on Yom Kippur, we read from the *Torah,* the five books of Moses. The scrolls are unrolled and are placed in the open for everyone to see. In this picture I am helping Rabbi Pil with the Torah, which is the most important of all Jewish scriptures. It contains the basic laws of Judaism and describes the ancient history of the Jews.

During a break in services, Rabbi Pil sits quietly with me and reads from the *Talmud,* a guide to the civil and religious laws of my faith. We talk about how lucky my family and I are to be able to practice our faith, and he talks to me about my future. On my thirteenth birthday I will read from the Torah in the synagogue and participate in the service. This is called a *bar mitzvah.* On that day I will become a man in the eyes of the Jewish community.

I feel very lucky that I now live in America and am able to live my life proudly and freely as an Orthodox Jewish boy.

Glossary

bar mitzvah (for a boy), *bat mitzvah* (for a girl). An important ceremony in the life of a Jewish child. It signifies the passage from childhood into adulthood. This occurs when a boy is thirteen years plus one day old. For girls, it is twelve years plus one day old.

challah. A rounded loaf of bread that is braided and smooth and served during Shabbat and festive meals.

Days of Awe. The High Holy Days (*yamin noraim*, in Hebrew): the ten days from Rosh Hashanah to Yom Kippur. These days are traditionally a time for a Jew to look at his or her life and make good on any wrongdoing that has been done during the past year.

émigré. A person who has to leave his or her country for political reasons.

fast. To go without some or all foods for a period of time.

kiddush. The prayer recited over wine on the evening of the Shabbat or on a holiday, before the start of the meal.

kosher. Clean or fit to eat according to the Jewish dietary laws.

l'chaim. Hebrew, literally "to life." A toast said before drinking.

rabbi. Title given to a spiritual teacher or leader of a Jewish community.

Rosh Hashanah. The Jewish New Year, presently celebrated in the fall on the first and second days of the Hebrew month of Tishri.

Shabbat. The seventh day of the week, Saturday; a holy day, a day of rest and relaxation from work.

shofar. The horn of a ram (or of any other ritually clean animal except for a cow), blown on Rosh Hashanah and Yom Kippur.

synagogue. A place where Jews come together to meet, to study, and to pray.

Talmud. Derived from a Hebrew word meaning "learning" or "study." It is a commentary on the Torah.

Tishri. The first month of the Jewish year.

Torah. The Five Books (Genesis, Exodus, Leviticus, Numbers, and Deuteronomy) that according to tradition were revealed to Moses by God on Mount Sinai.

tzedoka. Charity seen not as a favor to the poor but as something to which the needy have a right, and the donor an obligation.

tzitzis. Biblically prescribed fringes on the four corners of a garment worn under clothes by men and boys.

yarmulke. Skullcap worn by observant Jewish males.

Yom Kippur. The most solemn day of the Jewish religious year, culminating the ten Days of Awe that begin with Rosh Hashanah. Jews spend the entire day in fasting and prayer, asking forgiveness for all sins.

Sources

Dictionary of the Jewish Religion, Dr. Ben Issacson, SBS Publishing, 1979.

Jewish Family Celebrations: The Sabbath, Festivals and Ceremonies, Arlene Rossen Cardozo, St. Martin's Press, 1982.

Junior Judaica, Encyclopedia Judaica for Youth, Keter Publishing House, 1982.

Living Jewish: The Lore and Law of a Practicing Jew, Michael Asheri, Everest House, 1978.

My Jewish World, Robert Thum and Susan Dworski, Behrman House, 1989.